YOUR KNOWLEDGE HAS VALUE

- We will publish your bachelor's and
  master's thesis, essays and papers

- Your own eBook and book -
  sold worldwide in all relevant shops

- Earn money with each sale

Upload your text at www.GRIN.com
and publish for free

Bibliographic information published by the German National Library:

The German National Library lists this publication in the National Bibliography; detailed bibliographic data are available on the Internet at http://dnb.dnb.de .

Imprint:

Copyright © 2020 GRIN Verlag
Print and binding: Books on Demand GmbH, Norderstedt Germany
ISBN: 9783346123558

This book at GRIN:

https://www.grin.com/document/520650

Francisco Litvay

Software Startup Ecosystems. A Regional Comparison of Vienna and Zürich

GRIN Verlag

GRIN - Your knowledge has value

Since its foundation in 1998, GRIN has specialized in publishing academic texts by students, college teachers and other academics as e-book and printed book. The website www.grin.com is an ideal platform for presenting term papers, final papers, scientific essays, dissertations and specialist books.

Visit us on the internet:

http://www.grin.com/

http://www.facebook.com/grincom

http://www.twitter.com/grin_com

Submitted by

Francisco Litvay

Submitted at

**Department of Business
Informatics – Information
Engineering**

January 2020

SOFTWARE STARTUP ECOSYSTEMS

A Regional Comparison of Vienna and Zürich

Bachelor Thesis

to obtain the academic degree of

Bachelor of Science (/BSc)

in the Bachelor's Program

Business Informatics

TABLE OF CONTENTS

Abstract

The growth of software startups is highly dependent of the whole array of institutions and organizations surrounding them. The academic literature defines this environment as software startup ecosystem (SSE), or startup hub. Understanding the peculiarities and the maturity of specific SSEs allows founders to better comprehend what challenges they will be facing in their particular location, what advantages they have and what opportunities remain unexplored. SSE studies also allow other institutions, such as governmental agencies or support organizations, to understand which areas are most developed and which need more attention. This bachelor thesis seeks to analyze two regional central European SSEs, Zürich and Vienna, understand their differences, similarities and what one can learn from the other. To realize this, an analysis of both ecosystems' maturity was realized, using an existing SSE maturity model consisting of 22 metrics. This resulted in a classification of both SSE's maturity stages, which found Vienna to be nascent and Zürich to be mature.

1. Problem

1.1. Introduction

Software startups are important players in today's markets. According to Tripathi, Seppänen, et al. (2019), these firms contribute to job creation, innovation and economic growth at various levels. Their ability to attract vast sums of capital in short periods of time has positive impact on the locality they are headquartered, as part of this capital is used in demanding local products and services. For these reasons, many cities look for ways they can become more attractive for startups.

A critical factor for the creation and settling of new startups is it's environment, what the literature calls Software Startup Ecosystem (SSE), other variations being "entrepreneurial ecosystem" (Foster et al., 2013), "startup ecosystem" (Tripathi, Oivo, et al., 2019) and "innovation hub" (Sharma & Meyer, 2019). All these concepts address the multitude of actors and conditions present in a given region which impact entrepreneurship and startup development, such as pillar companies, research institutes, local governments and more. While the definitions vary, these often include the organizations mentioned before, along with mentorship and support institutions, such as incubators and accelerators, and existing entrepreneurship networks, such as founders and mentors.

These ecosystems can dramatically change the chances of success of early-stage startups, as they can provide them with more access to funding, talent, market reach and other relevant factors. In fact, Tripathi, Seppänen, et al. (2019) show that different startup ecosystem elements affect startups in every stage of their development, from conception to prototype development to delivery of functional products. Because of this, these ecosystems have become a hot topic for academic research, which is seeking to understand their characteristics and growth process by identifying key factors and analyzing their evolution over time.

1.2. Literature Review

A number of studies and books on startup/entrepreneurial ecosystems have been published. Queirós et al. (2019) analyze cross-country determinants of high-growth businesses, while De Bosco et al. (2019) investigate how local factors impact innovative startup creation. While studying innovation ecosystems, Bandera & Thomas (2018) have shown that there is a strong positive relationship between the utilization of an ecosystem's social capital and startup survival, especially for high tech companies.

Local analyses have also been a frequent topic, with Pandey (2018), Krajcik & Formanek (2015) and Motoyama & Watkins (2014) all studying their respective regional ecosystems. Case studies of this sort can help assess the strengths and weaknesses of existing ecosystems, as well as their maturity. By identifying key factors, research can show cities the direction they need to concentrate their efforts on and what type of initiatives need most promoting.

In "Software Startups - A Research Agenda" (Unterkalmsteiner et al., 2016), the authors explore the latest topics in the software startups research field. Section 3.5 specifically revolves around open research questions regarding Software Startups Ecosystems. RQ3 and RQ4, specifically, deal with the evolution and measurement of the outputs of SSEs. One existing issue was the lack of uniform definition of concepts and methodology among studies, which made comparisons between SSEs difficult, since there was no standard measurement and classification model. This has been noticed by a number of different researchers, which in parallel developed their own measurement models to evaluate SSEs.

When discussing the latest literature dealing with the evolution and measurement of SSEs, (Unterkalmsteiner et al., 2016) points to Cukier et al. (2015), who developed a maturity model for SSEs which was applied in the cities of Tel Aviv, Israel, and São Paulo, Brazil. At the time (2016), the model still needed validation. Cukier has since then finished his PhD work on this model and along with fellow researchers published a number of articles and papers on this model. The final version, with alterations improving a number of points, was published in 2018 (Cukier & Kon, 2018). Further case studies based on this model have been done for the city of Belo Horizonte (de Almeida & de Almeida, 2019), in Brazil, New York City (Cukier et al., 2016), in the US, and aspects of it such as its stages characterization has also found application in other countries, like India (Subrahmanya, 2017).

Further measurement models were developed by Sharma & Meyer (2019), Bell-Masterson & Stangler (2015) and Stam (2018). The following table provides an overview of their differences and similarities:

Factor	Cukier & Kon	Sharma & Meyer	Bell-Masterson & Stangler	Stam
Investigation focus	Software Startup Ecosystems	Innovation Hubs	Entrepreneurial Ecosystems	Entrepreneurial Ecosystems
Number of metrics	22	17	12	10
Number of countries investigated	3	0	0	1
Maturity levels per metric	3	5	None	None
Overall Maturity levels	4	5	None	None
Distinction between essential and secondary factors	Yes	No	No	No

Description of measurement criteria	Yes	No	Yes	Yes
Internet availability of data sources	Partial	Unknown	Partial	Total
Latest version	2013	2019	2015	2018

Table 1: Classification model comparison

The greatest difference between the models is that Cukier & Kon (2018) and Sharma & Meyer (2019) establish levels for individual metrics and general classifications based on these levels, while Bell-Masterson & Stangler (2015) and Stam (2018) present measurements for comparison without classification. These classifications allow researchers to track an ecosystem's evolution through time, as was done in Cukier et al. (2016). The subject of investigation also varies, with Sharma & Meyer (2019) focusing on the *Innovation Hub*, which in their definition is considered the central component of innovative Startup Ecosystems, Cukier & Kon (2018) focusing on *Software* (and more broadly *tech*) *Startup Ecosystems*, and Bell-Masterson & Stangler (2015) and Stam (2018) on the more general *Entrepreneurial Ecosystem*. Further, application require different amounts of effort by prospective appliers of the models. Stam (2018), for example, bases all metrics on indexes and statistics available online, while Cukier & Kon (2018) require personal questioning of individual stakeholders in the ecosystem.

1.3. Problem Definition and Validation

According to the Global Startup Ecosystem Report (Genome, 2019), which collected information from 1.000.000 companies and 150 startup ecosystems and ranked these based on 7 different criteria (Performance, Funding, Market Reach, Connectedness, Talent, Experience, and Knowledge), Austria does not have a single SSE ranked among the world's best. Vienna is the most active city in the country in that regard, accounting for half of the country's 1500 Startups founded since 2004 (Leitner et al., 2018), but it did not make the global ranks.

Austria's neighbor countries fare differently. Berlin, Germany, ranks 10th on top global SSEs. The German capital, however, has been on the global ranks since 2012 (Genome, 2012), and is a well-established ecosystem, making the validity and usefulness of comparisons between it and Vienna unreasonable. However, another of Austria's neighbors could shine a light on the way forward: Switzerland.

Switzerland has recently experienced an extraordinary growth in its startup landscape. According to Ankenbrand et al. (2019), Switzerland has already surpassed the United States in Company foundations per 10,000 capita since 2014, and this year the Lausanne-Bern-Geneva Startup Ecosystem ranked 22nd in the top 30 global ecosystems. In 2017, it was not even in the top 30, but in two years it was able to establish itself among the world's top 25 places for starting a startup.

Other sources recognize Austria as a regional European startup hub, but generally place it behind Switzerland. *Startup Ecosystem Rankings* (2019) recognized this, placing Switzerland as the 8th best ranked country, with Zürich taking the national 1st place. In comparison, Austria ranked 23rd in that classification, with Vienna as the national star. *Startup Heatmap Report* (2019) also recognizes both cities' as European hubs, with Vienna and Zürich ranking 13th and 14th place, respectively, with Zürich however outscoring Vienna in the individual classifications of Fintech, Biotech and Big Data.

Switzerland, like Austria, has experienced a large growth in its startup scene, especially in Bio-, Fintech and Blockchain, being able to successfully evolve and place itself as a global hub for startups in recent years. This begs the question of why this took place, considering both countries' similar geographical location, relative size and partly shared culture in the German-speaking cantons of Switzerland.

As the models in the literature review demonstrate, startup hubs are not national but rather regional phenomena, with very few cities and states usually concentrating most of a country's startup activity. As such, research is also mostly conducted on these specific areas – such as Silicon Valley, Berlin, Tel Aviv or greater São Paulo instead of more general USA, Germany, Israel and Brazil. Specific research of Austria's and Switzerland's leading SSE's would thus analyze Vienna and the canton of Zürich, which respectively hold 50 and 30% of their country's Startup activity (Kyora et al., 2018; Leitner et al., 2018).

1.4. Aims

This bachelor thesis seeks to analyze the Vienna and Zürich SSEs. By doing this analysis, this study will identify the differences and similarities between the Austrian and Swiss startup landscape, as well as discover what the most developed characteristics the ecosystems are and where they comparatively need the most improvement. This will be done by comparing Vienna's maturity level in various key factors to the canton of Zürich.

The intent of this analysis is both analytical and practical. Firstly, it seeks to evaluate if the Zürich ecosystem is indeed more mature than the Viennese, as the existing sources hint it to be. Secondly, it also aims at providing a practical overview of the areas in which the ecosystem's stakeholders should concentrate their efforts, by identifying areas lacking maturity which need attention, so that both SSEs can further develop and become more mature global startup hubs.

1.5. Research Questions

To fulfill the aims of this study, the following research question was formulated:

RQ1: What are the differences and similarities between the Vienna and the Zürich Software Startup Ecosystems?

To answer RQ1, the following two sub-questions have to be answered as well:

RQ1.1: How mature is Vienna's SSE?

RQ1.2: How mature is Zürich's SSE?

2. Methodology

The research questions were answered by a classification of the two SSE's based on the SSE Maturity Model (Cukier & Kon, 2018). This methodology choice is based on three reasons: Firstly, the completeness of the model, which analyses more factors than any other available model. Secondly, the focus of the model, which is set on Software (and more generally tech) Startups instead of more general entrepreneurial ecosystems, which is more fitting for business informatics related research. Lastly, the presence of existing case studies applying the model in different regions, which will allow for a maturity comparison between the two European SSEs and the other SSEs studied using the same criteria. This was done in section 4.2 of this study.

The application of Cukier & Kon's maturity model involves the analysis of 22 different criteria for each SSE with 3 possible levels of development, resulting in the classification of the two individual ecosystems in one of the four different stages of maturity.

2.1. Research Process

The Maturity Model is based on 22 metrics, each with 3 possible levels of development; L1, L2, and L3. 10 of these are considered essential factors. Out of the 22 metrics, 6 are based on global indexes and reports, while the others need to be investigated on a case by case basis, through the analysis of various reports, databases and also by personally contacting ecosystem stakeholders. The Ecosystem maturity model factor classification can be found in Table 2.

Ecosystem maturity model factor classification

Factor	L1	L2	L3
Exit strategies*	0	1	>=2
Global market*	<10%	10-40%	>40%
Entrepreneurship in universities*	<2%	2-10%	>10%
Culture values for entrepreneurship*	<0.5	0.5-0.75	>0.75
Startup events*	Monthly	Weekly	Daily
Ecosystem data and research*	N/A	Partial	Full
Ecosystem generations*	0	1	2
Mentoring quality	<10%	10-50%	>50%
Bureaucracy	>40%	10-40%	<10%
Tax burden	>50%	30-50%	<30%
Accelerators quality (% success)	<10%	1-50%	>50%
Access to funding in USD/year	<200M	200M to 1B	>1B
Human capital quality	>20th	15-20th	<15th
Technology transfer processes	<4.0	4.0-5.0	>5.0
Methodologies knowledge	<20%	20-60%	>60%
Specialized media players	<3	3-5	>5
Relatively measured factors (per 1 million inhabitants)			
Number of startups*	<200	200-1k	>1k

Angel funding in number of deals/year*	<5	5-50	>50
High-tech companies presence	<2	2-10	>10
Access to funding in number of deals/year	<50	50-300	>300
Incubators/tech parks	1	2-5	>5
Established companies influence	<2	2-10	>10

Table 2: Ecosystem maturity model factor classification (Cukier & Kon, 2018). * marks essential factors.

Based on these metrics, an SSE is on one of the following four maturity levels:

- Nascent (M1): A startup ecosystem still in its initial stages, with some local startups, but which has not yet seen global success.
- Evolving (M2): A startup ecosystem with some successful companies and regional impact. For this level, all essential factors need to be at least L2, while 30% of complementary factors need to be at least L2 as well.
- Mature (M3): A startup ecosystem with many successful companies with worldwide impact and a first generation of entrepreneurs who are helping it become self-sustainable. For this level, all essential factors need to be at least L2, 50% of complementary factors need to be at least L2 and 30% of all factors need to be on L3 as well.
- Self-sustainable (M4): A startup ecosystem which has become a global center hosting thousands of startups and with at least a second generation of entrepreneurs working on the long-term survivability of the ecosystem. For this level, all essential factors need to be at least L3, and 60% of complementary factors need to be L3 as well.

To satisfyingly evaluate the factors for the non-index-based metrics, e-mail interviews with individual ecosystem stakeholders took place, accompanied by a thorough review of the existing documents, data and literature on the SSEs of both countries/regions. Initial searches on Google Scholar for "Swiss Startup Ecosystem" and "Austrian Startup Ecosystem" led to the European Startup Monitor, by Kollmann et al. (2016). From there, partner organizations of the two countries in question were found.

For Austria, this led to AustrianStartups, which is one of the producers of the "Austrian Startup Monitor" (Leitner et al., 2018). The authors of the report were contacted per email. Further data sources and contacts for the study were discovered through snowballing – visiting organization partners and referenced studies as well as contacting recommended contact persons, until reaching *Ecosystem for start-ups in Vienna* (2019), which provided an overview of the Viennese ecosystem and its stakeholders. This overview document served as basis to finding further organizations, data and reports for Vienna.

For Switzerland, the European Startup Monitor led to Swiss Finance Startups and the Swiss Startups Association, which served as an initial point for searching ecosystem stakeholders for snowballing. Questioned contacts pointed to *Swiss Tech Startup Ecosystem* (2019), a map of Switzerland's tech startup ecosystem and its stakeholders. This overview document served as basis to finding further organizations, data and reports for Zürich.

Ecosystem stakeholders contacted by email received an explanation of the study and were asked to share their organization's experience regarding factors suitable to their respective organization type. For example, accelerators were asked about "accelerators quality" and universities about "entrepreneurship in universities", but not the other way around. The factors were accompanied by their definition as in Cukier & Kon (2018). Lastly, stakeholders were also asked to if they could point to other relevant sources or contact persons. In total, 11 organizations replied. The template email used can be found in the Appendix.

After this description of the general approach, the individual SSE's will be analyzed in the next section. First, Vienna's SSE will be classified based on the model. Then, the study will go over Zürich's classification. The results will be presented in section 3 and discussed in section 4 of this study.

2.2. Phase 1: Vienna SSE Maturity assessment

For exit strategies, the first criterion, there are four different options for successful startups: (a) profitable growth to the global market, (b) acquisition by a big company, (c) merge with another company, or (d) IPO. To find out how many of these are present, it is necessary to find out how many of these exit types already happened in the ecosystem. Regarding (a), according to Leitner et al. (2018), around 75% of Austrian startups have developed into international markets, and 42% are already "born global", targeting global markets from day one. Regarding (b) and (c), *Austrian Tech Exit Report* (2015) accounted for nearly 180 M&A deals in Austria, with around 40 of them coming from the IT & Tech sector, which saw its number of transactions almost double between 2012 and 2014. Thus, the sources indicate Austria as having >=2 exit options, ranking L3 on exit strategies.

The second criterion global market assesses the % of startups targeting global markets. According to Leitner et al. (2018), 70% of Startups are planning on offering services to foreign markets in the next 12 months, while 43% already do so. Being >40%, Austria ranks L3 on global markets.

Entrepreneurship in universities measures the percentage of alumni that founded a startup within 5 years of graduation. While this metric currently does not exist for Austria, a number of related metrics measured by Kailer et al. (2018) can help establish a classification. It does not show the actual % of founded companies, but rather the intention of doing so. In this context, 3,5% of Austrian students want to become founders directly after their studies, while 24,1% want to become founders five years after. Engineering, Computer Sciences/IT, Science of Art, Economics and Business all have higher than average intentions, with 32,9% of Computer Sciences/IT students and 36,1% of Science of art students leading the after five years intention list. Furthermore, 30% of the active entrepreneurs surveyed founded their start-up right after studies, while 51% founded their business more than 5 years ago. Given that students stick to their long-term intentions, the result for Austria is L3, surpassing the >10% bracket by 14,1%, with a 141% safety margin.

Mentoring quality measures the percentage of mentors that either had a successful startup in the past or founded and worked for more than 10 years in one or more startups. For the programs of the Wirtschaftsuniversität Wien, these numbers are estimated to be 60% for the first and 10-20% for the second criterion. Questioning other ecosystem stakeholders, revealed similar estimations for the ecosystem - around 50% for the first and 10% for the second criterion. In Accelerators and Incubators, that number is even higher, with some having exclusively mentors that fit one of the two criteria. Assuming other organizations have a similar percentage, the data would indicate a mentoring quality of >50%, placing Vienna on L3 in this metric.

Bureaucracy, tax burden and technology transfer process are all criteria based on indexes of the global competitiveness report. According to Schwab (2017), for Austria these are 21.3 and 51.6 for bureaucracy and tax burden, respectively, and an average of 5.3 for technology transfer process based on the business sophistication and innovation factors. This ranks Austria on L2 in bureaucracy, L1 in tax burden and L3 on technology transfer process.

Accelerators quality is measured by the percentage of startups in accelerators that reach the stage of receiving a next level investment or reach the global market in a sustainable profitable stage. Using publicly available data from some of the biggest accelerators that operate in Vienna, such as weXelerate, which accelerated +150 Startups, the Ventury Elevate, and A1 Campus, all accelerators which keep public data on alumni startups and members, the following results were found: 85 accelerated startups had their headquarters in Austria, 65 being in Vienna and 20 in other regions. Out of these, 23 were found to have received a next level investment or have reached global markets in a sustainable and profitable stage, 19 in Vienna and 4 in other regions ("*Startups*", n.d.; "Elevate Startup Acceleration", n.d.; "A1 Membership", n.d.; "A1 Partnership", n.d.). With 19 out of 65 accelerated startups fitting the criteria, the success rate equals 29,23% for the Viennese SSE, fitting in the 10-50% bracket and thus earning it a classification of L2 for this factor.

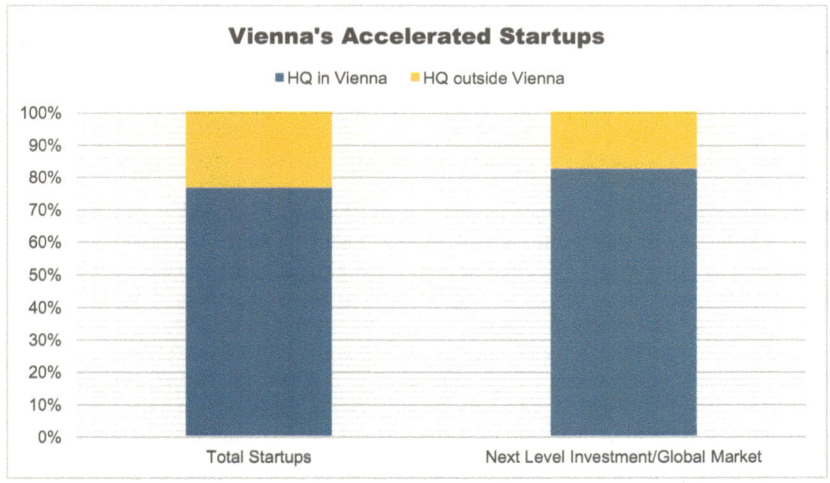

Figure 1: Austria's Accelerated Startups (Alumni or current accelerator members).

Access to funding is measured by the total amount of investment in startups in US$ according to a trusted database. According to Kandler (2018), the total amount of investment in Austrian Startups grew from 145 million in 2017 to 237 million in 2018, a 63% increase. This amount is in Euros, which converted to US Dollars totals roughly 262 million the time of this research. Non-Viennese Startups are credited with raising 39% of all capital in Austria, which leaves 61% in the hands of the Austrian capital, a total sum of roughly 160 million US dollars, leaving Vienna in the < 200M bracket of this factor, with a final classification of L1.

Human capital quality can be assessed by the ecosystem's position in the talent index of the global startup ecosystem report. Since Vienna is not among the top 20 ecosystems in the last 3 years (Genome, 2017; Genome, 2019), it must be concluded that its ranking is >20th, positioning Vienna in L1 for this metric.

Culture values for entrepreneurship can be found out through the Cultural support index in the Global Entrepreneurship and Development Index. According to Acs et al. (2018), this value for Austria is 0.683, which is between 0.5-0.75, positioning Austria in L2 for this metric.

Methodologies knowledge addresses the percentage of startups that have knowledge or are trained on systematic methodologies. As has been noted by Cukier & Kon (2018), this is a factor that is hard to measure. A thorough search of all reports and existing literature on the Austrian Startup scene revealed no hard data. The questioned startup ecosystem stakeholders also knew of no existing metric for the factor as well. The closest metric available is from Leitner et al. (2018), which includes data a survey questioning Austrian startups how innovative they consider themselves in relation to four aspects, one of which is "processes". While not a direct measure of companies adopting agile or systematic methodologies, the adoption of such methodologies is part of process innovation, *especially* for software startups. Data from the ASM Databank reveals the following picture: Out of an n = 437, 98 of the consider themselves innovative in relation to processes, while 114 considered themselves very innovative, the sum accounting for 48,5% of total startups surveyed. For the city of Vienna, the results are similar. Of 209 Viennese companies surveyed, 44 considered themselves employing innovative processes, while 51 considered themselves very innovative, resulting in a 44,24% total for the capital. This places Vienna in the 20-60% bracket, reaching an L2 classification in this factor. It is of note that incubators and similar supporting organizations contacted replied that either all or an estimated very high percentage of startups they engaged with had methodologies knowledge. However, there is not enough data from these sources to deem these samples as representative of the whole ecosystem.

The specialized media players metric counts the number of local media sources specialized in the startup industry and that are recognized by the local community. According to *Ecosystem for start- ups in Vienna* (2019), there are three such mediums covering the Startup and Tech Ecosystem in Austria: *Trending Topics*, *Der Brutkasten* and *Futurezone*. 3 specialized media players places Vienna in the 3-5 bracket, resulting in an L2 classification for this factor.

Startup events can be assessed by observing the frequency of local events on startup and high- tech entrepreneurship. For this, a research of all events happening in Vienna from the 1st of January of 2018 to the 31st of December of 2018 was conducted on the Austrian Startups event platform ("Event Calendar," n.d.). In total, the results were 43 events in January, 30 in February, 61 in March (with a considerable number of women in tech related events due to Women's day), 44 in April, 53 in May, 36 in June, 8 in July, 11 in August, 20 in September, 39 in October, 42 in November and lastly 16 in December. Most frequent among them are the weekly *Gründer Workshops* (Founder Workshops) by the WKO, and the events from the Wirtschafts Agentur Wien focused on founders.

Figure 2: Startup Events in Vienna.

It can be observed that on average there is more than an event per day, except on vacation months July, August and December. Despite the low average months, the total amount of events is 396 in the year of 2018, averaging 1,08 events daily. This classifies Vienna as L3 in this factor, due to having on average one startup event per day.

The ecosystem data and research metric addresses the existence of databases about the local startup ecosystem. The three categories are "N/A", „Partial" and „Full" when it comes to access to data. A thorough analysis of the ecosystem points us to three existing databases: ASM, Startablish and StartUs. The ASM database is based on the national survey conducted for the Austrian Startup Monitor report. However, only the final results on the report are available, as the database itself is not open to public use. Startablish, according to *Ecosystem for start-ups in Vienna* (2019), is a "real time databank that offers insights into austrian startups". With complete Startup profiles, charts measuring markets and industries, and data also available in a table format, Startablish is undoubtedly the most complete database of the Austrian Ecosystem. However, due to the acquisition of the Viennese Startup by brutkasten GmbH, a new version of the website is under development, meaning the database is unavailable at the time of this study. StartUs on the other hand is a website for networking, gathering job offers, organizational and professional profiles. It provides meaningful listings of the number and location of companies, accelerators, incubators, coworking spaces and so on, but has neither charting functions nor tables of the data. While not a database per se, it is currently the only available real-time online source for the Viennese SSE. Considering the available sources, the Viennese SSE ranks L2 with partial availability on this factor, as there are data sources, but which currently do not allow for a comprehensive data analysis. However, this factor must be reevaluated once the Startablish databank is made available to the public again, as this is likely to change the final result to L3 or full availability.

Ecosystem generations tracks the number of generations of prior entrepreneurs that are re-investing their earnings in the ecosystem. For this metric, person profiles on Crunchbase were analyzed using advanced search criteria (*Crunchbase*, n.d.). Two searches were made, one with location Austria and one with location Vienna. The search criteria included any persons who founded and invested or were partner investors in organizations headquartered in the SSE for the first search and on Austria for the second. 24 such individuals were found for Vienna, while 30 were found for Austria in total. Out of the 24 Vienna investor-founders, 4 of these were found to be investing in founders that are now themselves investing in the ecosystem. As such, Vienna has a solid existing 1st generation of founder-investors, but the 2nd generation is still in its early stage of formation. With an established 1st generation, the Austrian capital classifies as L2 for this metric.

Number of startups observes the number of startups founded per 1 million inhabitants. According to the ASM database (Leitner et al., 2018), in the years 2014, 2015, and 2016 (the last years for which complete data is available), Austria had 173, 227 and 227 startups founded each year, respectively, an average of 209 startups founded for the last three years. The country itself has 2.102 active Startups, with Vienna headquartering 1.087 of them, according to Crunchbase data (*Crunchbase*, n.d.). A division by 1.95 (Vienna's population in millions) results in 557 startups. This leaves Vienna in the 200-1k bracket, positioning it in L2 for this metric.

Access to funding and ange funding in deals per year can be assessed by the deal count for these two different categories. Kandler (2018), identified 101 deals in 2018, with 64 from them in Vienna. A division of this amount by Vienna's populations in millions results in 32 deals, placing Vienna in the < 50 bracket, resulting in a classification of L1. Out of the 64 deals, 8 of them can be classified as coming from angel investors (company, PhagoMed, twingz, Yodel, myBioma, MOOCI, Sheepblue and WisR). Divided by 1.95, the result is 4.1 angel deals per year. Further, according to Dealroom, Vienna saw in total 4 angel funding rounds in 2019 and 12 angel funding rounds in the last 3 years, an average of 4 yearly (*Dealroom.co*, n.d.). Divided by the Vienna's population in millions (1.95), this results in a relative number of 2 angel deals/year. Thus, both sources place Vienna in the < 5 bracket, scoring an L1 in this factor as well.

The incubators/tech parks metric tracks the number of active incubators and tech parks in the ecosystem. According to Siegl (2019b), there are in total 10 such institutions active in Vienna. Since this is a relative factor, it must be divided by the number of inhabitants of Vienna in millions (1.95), resulting in a relative value of 5.12. This places Vienna in the >5 bracket, resulting in a classification of L3 for this factor.

For the high-tech company presence metric, research needs to find out the number of high-tech established companies with tech teams located in the ecosystem region. Research for this metric consisted of two steps: First, locating high-tech companies with at least national influence which have offices in Vienna. The established companies list and definition from the "established companies influence" metric was used (see below), supplemented with the many documents from ABA, such as Siegl (2017c, 2017d, 2017b, 2017a, 2019a) which provide lists of foreign and local companies in Austria from a number of high-tech industries, such as Industry 4.0, ICT and Life Sciences. The second step consisted of finding out which of these companies were headquartered or had tech teams in the regions. For the headquarters, individual searches through the companies' websites were conducted, locating headquarters locations. For tech-teams, the same procedure was repeated, this time searching for branch offices. Searches through the company's career platforms were performed, looking for tech-related and operational positions in the area. This was done to exclude offices dedicated solely to customer support and leave only those in which research or development teams are active. A total of 17 high-tech established companies were found to either be based in Vienna or have headquarters in the city with a tech team. These are A1, Magenta (Telecommunications), Andritz (Engineering), TTTech, Atos, Frequentis, Kapsch (ICT), Raiffeisen Bank International, Erste, Bawag, paysafecard (Banking and Payments), Verbund (Energy), Deloitte (Risk management), Siemens (Conglomerate), Boehringer, Shire (Pharmaceuticals) and Otto Bock (R&D and Prosthetics). The total of 17 companies divided by

Vienna's population in millions (1.95) results in a relative metric of 8.7, placing Vienna in the 2-10 bracket. Thus, Vienna classifies as L2 for high-tech company presence.

Lastly, the established companies influence metric delivers the number of pillar companies that have activities focused on the ecosystem's growth. For this, large corporations with at least national influence that support local organizations need to be analyzed. A backward search was made by searching companies that supported organizations and events mentioned in *Ecosystem for start-ups in Vienna* (2019). This included partnering with and directly sponsoring the Austrian Startup scene, including directly supporting organizations such as AustrianStartups, events such as Pioneers and accelerators such as weXelerate. To be considered an active supporter of the ecosystem, a company had to either support multiple initiatives at the normal level or be the main sponsor or organizer for one of them. Then, the remaining established companies with national or international influence were selected, 16 in total. These are A1, Andritz, Erste Group, Frequentis, Palfinger, Post, Magenta, Raiffeisen Bank International, Red Bull, Delloite, Infineon, Google, Strabag, Uniqa Insurance Group, Bawag PSK and Verbund. Divided by Vienna's population in millions (1.95), this results in a relative number of 8.2. This result places Vienna in the 2-10 bracket, classifying as L2 in this metric.

2.3. Phase 2: Zürich's SSE Maturity assessment

For exit strategies, the first criterion, there are four different options for successful startups: (a) profitable growth to the global market, (b) acquisition by a big company, (c) merge with another company, or (d) IPO. To find out how many of these are present, it is necessary to find out how many of these exit types already took place in the ecosystem. Regarding (a), (b) and (c), according to Kurth (2019), 2018 saw 230 deals of Swiss enterprises either acquiring or merging with foreign targets, while 117 deals of foreign enterprises either acquiring or merging with Swiss targets were recorded, showing that while all of the options mentioned are possible, Swiss growth to international markets is twice more likely than M&As from foreign companies. As for IPOs, Heimann & Kyora (2019) records four Zürich IPOs – Sensirion, Medartis, Polyphor and Asmallworld. Thus, the sources indicate Switzerland as having >=2 exit options, ranking L3 on exit strategies.

The second criterion global market assesses the % of startups targeting global markets. According to "Global market at a glance" (n.d.), "Swiss start-ups plan for the global market right from the start. As soon as they are able to bring products or services to the market, they expand abroad: 60% of companies export after only three years, and that share rises to 80% after 10 years". When calculated with Startup.ch's Startup Index (*Startup.ch*, n.d.), using the most conservative estimations based on the data – that year 1-2 has 0% exports, year 3-9 have 60% exports and 10+ have 80% – research reaches the numbers shown in Figure 3.

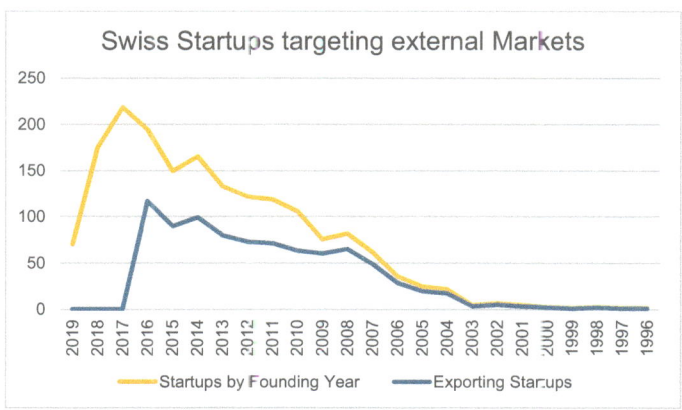

Figure 3: Swiss Startups targeting external Markets.

With a total of 1765 startups listed and 844 already exporting, Switzerland reaches 47,8% of startups targeting global markets, thus ranking L3 on global markets.

Entrepreneurship in universities measures the percentage of alumni that founded a startup within 5 years of graduation. Similarly as for Austria, this metric currently does not exist, but a number of related metrics measured by Sieger et al. (2018) can help establish a classification. Just like the Austrian national GUESS report, it does not show the actual % of founded companies, but rather the intention of doing so. In this context, 2,3% of Swiss students want to become founders directly after their studies, while 20,1% want to become founders five years after. Engineering, Computer Sciences/IT, Science of Art, Economics and Business students all have higher than average intentions, with 31,9% of Computer Sciences/IT students and 38,1% of Science of Art students leading the after five years intention list. Furthermore, 72,4% of students said they want to become founders directly after their studies have already founded or are in the process of founding their own company. This number equals 9.3% for those who plan on founding a company in the next five years. Given that students stick to their long-term intentions, the result for Switzerland is L3, surpassing the >10% bracket by 10,1%, with a 101% safety margin.

Mentoring quality measures the percentage of mentors that either had a successful startup in the past or founded and worked for more than 10 years in one or more startups. According to VentureLab, one of the biggest national startup training programs, this metric depends on the startup being supported. The organization hires both more experienced trainer-entrepreneurs, as well as younger and more recent founders that have very successful startups. According to them, this combines the best of both worlds, since older generations usually have deeper insights into a specific industry and bigger networks, while younger entrepreneur-trainers usually have better insights into current marketing activities and funding experience. In any case, for the Innosuisse Startup-Training, also organized by VentureLab, every trainer has actual startup experience and normally went through one of their programs before. So, although there is no objective metric of all mentors, Innosuisse's and VentureLab's experience demonstrate that the majority of mentors fit one of the two criteria. As such, the classification for Zürich would be >50%, or L3.

Bureaucracy, tax burden and technology transfer process are all criteria based on indexes of the global competitiveness report. According to Schwab (2017), for Switzerland these are 19.0 for bureaucracy, 28.8 for tax burden and an average of 5.9 for technology transfer process based on the business sophistication and innovation factors. This ranks Switzerland on L2 in bureaucracy, L3 in tax burden and L3 in technology transfer process.

Accelerators quality is measured by the percentage of startups in accelerators that reach the stage of receiving a next level investment or reach the global market in a sustainable profitable stage. Using data from accelerators that operate in Zürich, such as Kickstart-Innovation, which accelerated +130 Startups, and VentureLab, another accelerator that keeps public data on alumni startups and supported businesses, the following results were found: Out of a total of 264 accelerated startups, 112 met the criteria of a next level investment or having successfully reached global markets (*Kickstart » Alumni*, n.d.), (*Swiss Startups—Venturelab*, n.d.). From these 264, 135 were in Zürich, with 57 meeting the criteria explained above, resulting in a success rate of 42,22%. This places Zürich in the 10-50% bracket, earning it an L2 rank for this factor.

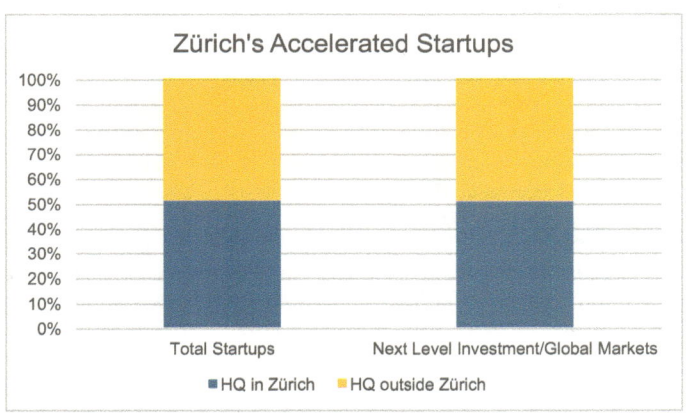

Figure 4: Zürich's Accelerated Startups.

Access to funding is measured by the total amount of investment in startups in US$ according to a trusted database. According to the latest Swiss Venture Capital Report (Heimann & Kyora, 2019), in 2018 a total sum of 515.2 million CHF was invested in Startups in Zürich, an incredible 71% increase from 2012. As of the date of this study, this sum totals 520.18 million US dollars. This places Zürich in the 200M to 1B bracket, earning Zürich an L2 classification in this factor.

Human capital quality can be assessed by the ecosystem's position in the talent index of the global startup ecosystem report. Since Zürich is not among the top 20 ecosystems in the last 3 years (Genome, 2017; Genome, 2019), we must conclude that its ranking is >20th, positioning it in L1 for this metric. One could assume that since Lausanne-Bern-Geneva makes the ranking, that Zürich would have a similar human capital quality as well. However, the latest report (Genome, 2019) no longer classifies ecosystems by positions, but by *tiers.* This means that the *Talent* index is divided into 5 different tiers, from 1st (best) to 5th. Dividing the tiers by the number of positions and comparing them to the classifiers, means that 1st (1-6) and 2nd (7-12) tier are L3, 3rd (13-18) tier is L2-L3, 4th (19-24) tier is L1-L2 and 5th (25-30) tier is L1. Lausanne-Bern-Geneva ranks 5th, positioning it in L1. This means that even if Zürich had the same capital quality as its Swiss neighbor cities, the capital quality factor would still be L1 according to these criteria.

Culture values for entrepreneurship can be found out through the cultural support index in the Global Entrepreneurship and Development Index. According to Acs et al. (2018), this value for Switzerland is 0.673, which is between 0.5-0.75, positioning Switzerland in L2 for this metric.

Methodologies knowledge addresses the percentage of startups that have knowledge or are trained on systematic methodologies. As stated in the original model from Cukier & Kon (2018) and in the Vienna SSE assessment section, this is a particularly hard factor to measure. The most similar metric that could be found for the Swiss Startup Ecosystem was the % of startups that are engaging in process innovation, which totals 35% for Switzerland, according to *Discover (Einblicke in das Jahr 2018 von Innosuisse*, 2019). This places the SSE on the 20-60% bracket, reaching a classification of L2 for this metric. Noteworthy is that similarly to Vienna, accelerators and incubator programs reported that most if not all of their startups had knowledge of systematic methodologies.

The specialized media players metric counts the number of local media sources specialized in the startup industry and that are recognized by the local community. *Swiss Tech Startup Ecosystem* (2019) lists in total three: *Startwerk, Startupticker* and *Fintecnnews*. This places Switzerland in the 3-5 bracket, positioning the country in L2 for this metric.

Startup events can be assessed by observing the frequency of local events on startup and high-tech entrepreneurship. Some websites, such as StartupTicker (*Events Startupticker.ch*, n.d.), aggregate data on upcoming events, but none has the completeness which can be found in Vienna's AustrianStartups website. This makes assessing the total number of events more difficult for people engaged in Switzerland's startup ecosystem. *Swiss Tech Startup Ecosystem* (2019) lists 17 different event organizations in Switzerland. Out of these, 12 (Finance 2.0, Digital Festival (2x per year), StartupGrind (around 10 per year), StartupCampus, StartupNight, VentureDay, Entrepreneur Club (around 20 per year), Impact Sprints, Energy Startup Day, IPO Day, Startup Weekend, SICTIC (around 22 per year)) do on average 62 Startup and high-tech related events per year in the canton of Zürich. Other platforms like StartupTicker records 6 events for January, while Eventbrite (a general event platform) records 11 (*Eventbrite*, n.d.). Even if this sum were to be multiplied by 12 (which is an unrealistic assumption, since July, August and December are considerably under the monthly average), the total number of events would amount to 266, a 99 event difference to the 365 yearly average required for there to be a daily event occurrence. Thus, Zürich falls under the "weekly" startup event occurrence bracket, with an L2 classification for this factor.

The ecosystem data and research metric addresses the existence of databases about the local startup ecosystem. Switzerland has a good number of databases regarding their ecosystem. Switzerland Global Enterprise has a business navigator with business data, dynamic maps, comparisons and more (*Business Navigator*, n.d.). Startup.ch has a Startup radar keeping track of all startups, which can be looked up by location, founding date, sector and other criteria, but has less total numbers than Crunchbase. (*Startup.ch*, n.d.). SwissStartups aggregates accelerators, incubators, coworking spaces, investors and other Startup ecosystem actors (*SwissStartups.org*, n.d.). Spied keeps track of ETH Spinoffs (*Spin-off Information ETHZ, EPFL, PSI, WSL, Empa, Eawag*, n.d.). There are also various databases of specific branches in the country. Cryptovalley has a detailed directory of the Blockchain ecosystem (*CryptoValley Swiss Blockchain Ecosystem*, n.d.). The Swiss Finance + Tech Association keeps track of the Fintech ecosystem with their own directory ("Ecosystem Directory," n.d.), while the Swiss Environment & Energy Innovation Monitor lists all startups involved in the Environment and Energy sectors (*Innovation Monitor*, n.d.). Due to this variety of different sources, one must consider the Swiss ecosystem as one with full coverage of ecosystem data, earning it an L3 classification.

Ecosystem generations tracks the number of generations of prior entrepreneurs that are re-investing their earnings in the ecosystem. For this metric, person profiles on Crunchbase were analyzed using advanced search criteria (*Crunchbase*, n.d.). Two searches were made, one with location Switzerland and one with location Zürich. The search criteria included any which founded and invested or were partner investors in organizations headquartered in the SSE for the first search and on Switzerland for the second. 34 such individuals were found for Zürich, while 87 were found for Switzerland in total. Out of 34 investor-founders from Zürich, 3 were found to be investing in founders who are themselves now investing in Zürich startups. Zürich too has a solid existing 1st generation of founder-investors, with the beginnings of a 2nd generation in sight. With an established 1st generation, the Swiss canton classifies as L2 for this metric.

Number of startups observes the number of startups founded by year per 1 million inhabitants. According to the Startup.ch database, there were 194 Startups founded in Zürich in 2016, 149 in 2015, and 165 in 2014, an average of 169 for the three years. According to Crunchbase, Switzerland has 11,733 active startups, with Zürich headquartering 3,439 of them (*Crunchbase*, n.d.). Divided by its population in millions (1.52), the relative metric is 2262 Startups founded in Zürich, placing it in the >1k bracket. This earns Zürich an L3 classification in this factor.

Access to funding and angel funding in deals per year can be assessed by the deal count for these two different categories. According to Heimann & Kyora (2019), the canton of Zürich was responsible for a total of 99 funding rounds in the year of 2018, out of 230 funding rounds in Switzerland. Divided by its population in millions (1.52), the relative metric is 65 deals in the year of 2018, placing Zürich in the 50-300 bracket, with a final classification of L2. According to Dealroom, Zürich saw in total 8 angel funding rounds in 2019 and 23 angel funding rounds in the last 3 years, an average of 7.66 yearly (*Dealroom.co*, n.d.). Divided by the Zürich population in millions (1.52), the study finds a relative number of 5.04 angel deals/year, placing Zürich in the 5-50 bracket and earning it a classification of L2 for this factor.

The incubators/tech parks metric tracks the number of active incubators and tech parks in the ecosystem. *Swiss Tech Startup Ecosystem* (2019) has tracked the active incubators and tech parks in the Swiss Startup Ecosystem, 41 in total. Out of these, 16 are in Zürich. Divided by its population in millions (1.52), the result is a relative number of 10 incubators and tech parks, exceeding the >5 bracket and thus earning Zürich an L3 classification for this metric.

For the high-tech company presence metric, research needs to find out the number of high-tech established companies with tech teams located in the ecosystem region. Research was conducted using the same methodology for Vienna, consisting of two steps and using the initial established companies list from "established companies influence". The list was supplemented with other high-tech companies mentioned on Switzerland Global Enterprise's factsheets on different branches, such as Fintech (*Fintech Switzerland*, 2019), ICT (*Switzerland—ICT Business Location*, 2019), Robotics (*Switzerland—A Hub for Robotics and Drones*, 2019), Biotech (*Biotech Cluster in*

Switzerland, 2019), Blockchain (*Blockchain Hub Switzerland*, 2019) and more, which describe the Swiss market for the branch and map high-tech companies of these branches active in the region. All companies' websites and career platforms were then inspected to discover their headquarters locations and branch offices with active tech teams. 24 such companies were found to be present in Zürich. The ones mapped for this research are Molecular Partners AG, Neurimmune (Biotech), Teccan Group, ABB, Bosch Mettler Toledo, Amazon, Roche, Dacadoo, ABB, Siemens (Robotics), AdNovum, Avaloq, ELCA, Google, IBM, Microsoft, Netcetera, Noser Group, Swisscom, Disneystudios (ICT), AdNovum, Crealogix and SIX (Fintech). Divided by Zürich's population in millions (1.52), the relative metric for high-tech companies is 15, belonging in the >10 bracket and thus earning Zürich a classification of L3 for this factor.

Lastly, the established companies influence metric delivers the number of pillar companies that have activities focused on the ecosystem's growth. Once more, large companies that support local startup-related organizations were analyzed using the same backward search methodology used in the Vienna analysis, but this time with the sources from (*Swiss Tech Startup Ecosystem*, 2019). Companies actively supporting multiple initiatives at the normal level or being the main sponsor or organizer of one initiative were investigated. This support included partnering with and sponsoring event-organizers such as Startup Grind, news sources such as StartupTicker, supporting incubators and accelerators, as well as associations such as SICTIC. 18 established companies with at least national presence could be tracked as fitting this categorization: Google, IBM, SAP BDO, Die Post, Randstad, Thomson Reuters, Swisscom, KPMG, Generali, Six Group, Zürcher Kantonalbank, UBS, Helvetia, Mobiliar, Zühlke, Axpo and Credit Suisse. Divided by Zürich's population in millions (1.52), the relative metric equals 11 influential established companies placing Zürich in the >10 bracket and thus classifying as L3 for this factor.

3. Results

This section presents the classifications of the two SSE's for each of the analyzed factors, as well as their overall maturity level.

Startup ecosystem comparison table

Factor	Vienna	Zürich
Exit strategies*	L3	L3
Global market*	L3	L3
Entrepreneurship in universities*	L3	L3
Culture values for entrepreneurship*	L2	L2
Startup events*	L3	L2
Ecosystem data and research*	L2	L3
Ecosystem generations*	L2	L2
Mentoring quality	L3	L3
Bureaucracy	L2	L2
Tax burden	L1	L3

Accelerators quality (% success)	L2	L2
Access to funding in USD/year	L1	L2
Human capital quality	L1	L1
Technology transfer processes	L3	L3
Methodologies knowledge	L2	L2
Specialized media players	L2	L2
Relatively measured factors (per 1 million inhabitants)		
Number of startups*	L2	L3
Angel funding in number of deals/year*	L1	L2
High-tech companies presence*	L2	L3
Access to funding in number of deals/year	L1	L2
Incubators/tech parks	L3	L3
Established companies influence	L2	L3
Essential Factors	L3 (4), L2 (5), L1(1)	L3 (6), L2 (4)
Complementary Factors	L3 (3), L2 (6), L1 (3)	L3 (5), L2 (6), L1 (1)
Maturity Level	Nascent (M1)	Mature (M3)

Table 3: Startup Ecosystem Comparison table. *Essential Factors

4. Discussion

4.1. SSE comparison – Vienna and Zürich

In this section, the individual factors and the final classifications will be discussed. Eventual shortcomings in data availability will also be laid out.

First, **exit strategies.** In this criterium, both ecosystems were found to be well developed, with a sizeable percentage of companies targeting global markets (more on this below) and mergers & acquisitions taking place regularly in the ecosystem. While there is no one source of data for the individual ecosystems on M&As, national data already presents a decent overview of the situation: Although both countries ranked L3, Switzerland saw a higher total number of M&A deals – 230 to Austria's 180. Still, it would be useful for comparing the ecosystems to know if the deal amount proportions hold stable between the canton of Zürich and the city of Vienna, since it may be the case that the local numbers do not reflect the national numbers.

Regarding **global markets**, both countries proved to be highly internationalized, reaching the L3 factor. This can be in part assumed to be due to the countries' small domestic markets, which increases the incentive to internationalize. While Brazilian or American companies have a large possible customer base in their own countries, due to their countries' massive population, the same does not hold true for the Swiss and Austrians. Austria's membership in the European Union and Switzerland's membership in the European Single Market can also be seen as factors leading to internationalization, since these greatly reduce the hurdle of reaching European markets. One shortcoming regarding this factor's trustworthiness is that there is no hard empirical data on Zürich's or the Swiss ecosystem for the percentage of companies that *currently* target global markets. The only source found reporting on Swiss companies' export tendencies gave statistics for after years 3 and 10 of founding. Because of this, the number used for classification is an application of this statistic "rule" to the number of startups founded by year. Although the estimation used conservative numbers (such as assuming that 0% of startups export in years 1-3) and still reached the most mature classification with a 7,8% safety margin, a more detailed study could be conducted to find out the actual value for this criterion.

When it comes to **entrepreneurship in universities**, both countries surpass the >10% bracket of student founders after 5 years, with 24,1% of Austrian students wanting to be come founders after 5 years of graduation. In comparison, 20,1% of Swiss students plan on doing the same, a 3% difference. The national reports from the GUESS surveys unfortunately do not present the percentages for individual institutions, which could have allowed for a comparison between the values for higher education institutions in Vienna and Zürich. Furthermore, the report gives no feedback from what students said they would do and what they actually did once the 5 years had passed, which would allow researchers to estimate how likely students are to act on their intentions during university in each country. These two points, if incorporated into future GUESS studies, would greatly increase the accuracy of this research.

Culture values for entrepreneurship, unlike the previous factor, is straightforward and leaves little room for accuracy in its collection, since it requires only a look up at the cultural support index in the Global Entrepreneurship and Development Index. In this factor, both countries classify as L2, but Austria has a slightly higher value of 0.683, a 0.010 difference to Switzerland's 0.673.

Regarding **startup events**, Vienna has the upper hand. With more events, trainings and meetups then there are days of the year, the Austrian capital almost always has some startup or high-tech related event taking place. Zürich doesn't fare badly either, since the canton's SSE also has a variety of high-value events, averaging around one per week. Worth mentioning for this factor is the ease of discovering new events: While Switzerland has several event organizations, there is no single website which aggregates data on all future and past events and lets the user search through them using different criteria, like AustrianStartups does. The closest in the Swiss SSE is StartupTicker's event platform, but it lacks relevant events from Eventbrite and a past events search function. The Austrian platform also allows for different visualization modes, search by keywords and has more event categories than its Swiss equivalent. Regarding the factor itself, a more exact definition would improve the objectivity. Current classifications are named "Daily, Weekly, Monthly", but it is not clear exactly what numbers belong to each range. Two definitions can be considered: One would be "*at least daily/weekly/monthly*", while the other would be "*closer to daily/weekly/monthly*". Depending on which is used, the ranges for each maturity level vary drastically. For the first, L1 would be [0-51], L2 would be [52-364] and L3 [>364]. For the second, L1 would be [0-32], L2 would be [33-208] and L3 [>208]. Luckily the results for Vienna and Zürich are remain the same with both definitions, but for further studies that may not be the case, which is why this study recommends formally adopting either one of them for next versions of the maturity model.

The **ecosystem data and research** factor determined Switzerland's SSE as being more mature than Austria, with the country scoring an L3 in comparison to its neighbor's L2. It is worth noting that both countries are very well off in terms of reports of the SSE's situation and in providing documents for interested parties, with several organizations engaged in producing such content for both countries. Switzerland's SSE has been classified as having full data availability due to the availability of open data sources, such as Startup.ch's extensive list of Startups and investors and Switzerland Global Enterprise's business navigator including key figures, among other websites. Austria also has two extensive databanks, the ASM Databank and Startablish. However, since the former is not open to public access, and the latter is under maintenance as to the date of this study, this leaves researchers with no Austrian databases on the SSE, making Austria's data availability partial for the time being.

Ecosystem generations tracks the number of generations of prior entrepreneurs reinvesting their earnings in the ecosystem. Two metrics are related to this factor: The number of persons who founded companies in the SSE and the number of persons that founded *and* did investments or were partners in investments in the SSE. According to Crunchbase, the total number of Vienna founders is 793, compared to Zürich's 1,258. Out of the 793 Vienna founders, 24 were found to be reinvesting in the ecosystem, and out of the 24, 4 had already invested in founders who themselves invested in the ecosystem. Since the 4 founders with 2 generations are a subset of the 24 founders with one generation and the 24 a subset of the founders with 0 generations, a proportion calculation needs to remove the double counting of generation 1 and 2 investor-founders. With that done, the proportion of founders in generation 2, 1 and 0 in Vienna is 1:5:193, that is, for every generation 2 founder-investor, there are 5 generation 1s and around 193 generation 0s. In Zürich, 34 founders were identified as re-investing in the ecosystem, with 3 of them having invested in founders who are themselves re-investing in the ecosystem. For Zürich, the proportion of generation 2, 1 and 0 founders is then 1:10:408. Thus, it is possible to identify in Zürich a larger basis of founders and 1st generation investor-founders, but Vienna slightly surpasses the Swiss canton on the number of 2nd generation investor-founders, both in absolute as well as in relative numbers. In both ecosystems, there is an existing established first generation of founders-investors, with a next generation starting to appear. It is of note that for this criterion there is no defined objective measure of what constitutes a whole generation – if it is an absolute number or a % of entrepreneurs, for example. Further refinements of the SSE maturity model could include an objective measurement basis.

When it comes to **mentoring quality,** both countries have a high percentage of mentors that have experience in the startup scene, be it by either being a successful founder or by working on the field for years. For this definition of mentoring quality there is neither an objective international index nor data from national reports, so this data had to be collected by personally contacting organizations that provide mentoring. While data from established and renowned institutions from both SSEs were used, further research (preferentially national reports like the ASM) could include these metrics to have more accurate data from both SSEs. Alternatively, adoption of a global index for this metric could facilitate future case studies. Although the author of this document does not see an exact equivalent, one possibility would be the combination of the "Networking" Pillar present in Acs et al. (2018) with another metric evaluating entrepreneur's experience.

Bureaucracy analyzed the percentage of respondents that classified bureaucracy as the most problematic factor of doing business. For this factor, both countries are in the 10-40% bracket, reaching a classification of L2. Switzerland has a slightly less bureaucratic system, scoring 19.0% to Austria's 21.3%. However, in Switzerland bureaucracy is perceived by the respondents to be the most problematic factor for doing business, while in Austria bureaucracy is 2nd to "Restrictive Labor regulations", which scored 23.2%. While bureaucracy certainly remains a problem for both countries, both also have competent institutions that provide assistance to prospective founders and foreign companies in establishing themselves in the respective countries, such as ABA in Austria and Swiss Global Enterprise in Switzerland (*How to start a Business in Austria*, n.d.; *Company foundation in Switzerland*, n.d.).

Tax burden is one of the factors in which the difference between the two countries is starkest. This variable, according to Schwab (2017), is a combination of the profit tax, labor tax, contribution and other taxes as a % of profits. Switzerland has very low taxes, ranking 31st out of the 137 countries analyzed with 28.8% total taxes as percentage of profits. Austria, on the other hand, ranks 113th of all countries analyzed, with 51.6% total taxes as percentage of profits. Analyzing the data shows that Austria's score is 79% higher than that of Switzerland, placing the country in the world's least attractive quartile in this aspect, with Switzerland in the most attractive quartile.

When it comes to **accelerators quality**, both SSE's are on the same maturity level (L2), but Zürich still takes the lead with a 10% higher success rate. The graphs presented for both SSE's measure the relative success of accelerated startups headquartered in the SSE and in other regions of the country. However, the differences in the % of total startups headquartered in the SSE does not necessarily represent the proportions of total startups of the country. The considerably higher percentage of total startups seen in the Vienna as compared to Zürich, for example, is partly due to the weXelerate accelerator operating only in Vienna and Dornbirn, while ventureLab, which provided most of the data for Switzerland, operates in Zürich, Lausanne and St. Gallen. What is relevant in the graphs is the % of successful startups in relation to the % of total startups recorded. In that regard, the percentages for Zürich are even, while Vienna is overrepresented in regard to successful accelerated startups. It is of note that no hard definition of "next-level investment" is provided. For this study, funding of at least near 1€ million was used. A standard definition, be it simple or in relation to national metrics, could help make further case studies more objective.

Access to funding in USD/year shows the maturity of the Zürich SSE (and the Swiss SSE, in general). The leading Swiss canton attracted impressive 520 million US$ in investment in 2018, fitting in the 200 million to 1 Billion interval of L2. Switzerland in total attracted 1259 million US$, making its leading canton responsive for 41,3% of invested capital in Startups. Vienna has a large share of the "national pie", attracting 61% of Startup capital in Austria, but the Austrian pie is smaller, totaling 262 million US$, leaving the Austrian capital with roughly 160 million US$, less than a third of the amount attracted in Zürich. Thus Vienna, by attracting less than 200 million US$, scores L1 in this factor. A similar percentage distribution between the two SSE's can also be seen below in "Access to funding in number of deals/year".

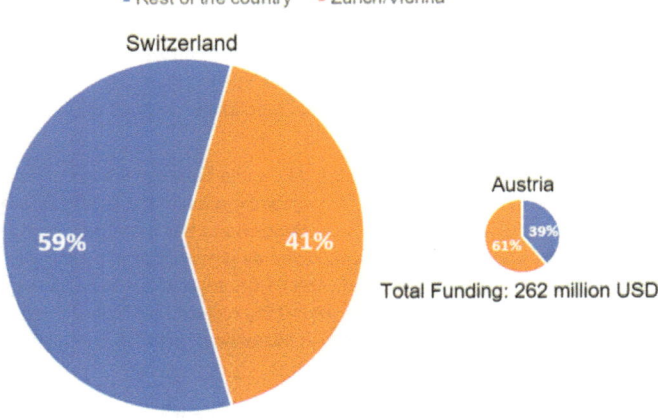

Funding in Switzerland and Austria in 2018

■ Rest of the country   ● Zürich/Vienna

Switzerland

59%   41%

Total Funding: 1259 million USD

Austria

61%   39%

Total Funding: 262 million USD

Figure 5: Funding in Switzerland and Austria in 2018

Human capital quality is one of the few factors in which both SSE's score an L1. However, one cannot assume from this classification that the quality of human capital in Vienna and Zürich is bad. This factor in specific is the only one in the classification which is based on an ordinal number – that is, which doesn't classify the SSE by its own properties, but by its performance in relation to other SSEs. To make matters worse, the report from which classification in this factor is derived only includes the top 30 SSEs worldwide, which severely limits ecosystems which are not yet global stars to be considered to have a high human capital quality, further reducing the usefulness of this factor for analyzing SSEs which are not already in the global spotlights. This creates a strange "fixed-pie" scenario, in which even if every single SSE in the world saw a 100x increase in its human capital, the maturity in this factor for all of them would be considered exactly the same. Improving Cukier and Kon's SSE Maturity model by using a similar metric with cardinal values or percentages and that includes more than only 30 ecosystems would solve this issue. The author suggests the "Skills" pillar in Schwab (2019) as an alternative. The latest version of the Global Competitiveness report includes a new performance pillar, "Skills", which analyses the mean years of schooling and the skills of the current workforce, as well as the school life expectancy and skills of the future workforce. This an absolute value with data for 141 countries, making this metric a suitable substitute.

Technology transfer processes shows that both countries are very mature when it comes to business sophistication and innovation, with both countries having a value higher than 5.0 and thus reaching L3 in this metric. When it comes to the exact numbers, Austria has a business sophistication of 5.6 and innovation of 5.0, resulting in an average of 5.3. Meanwhile, Switzerland has a business sophistication of 5.9 and innovation of 5.8, resulting in an average of 5.9. Thus, Switzerland slightly outperforms Austria in business sophistication, outperforms Austria in innovation by a larger margin (0.8 instead of 0.3) and thus outperforms Austria overall in technology transfer processes.

In **methodologies knowledge**, both SSEs are considered to be in the same maturity level. Vienna was found to have a 20% higher methodologies knowledge when compared to Zürich for the given data. This factor, however, is the least trustworthy of this study, as the metric used only correlates indirectly with the desired metric. Further surveys from both ecosystems could ask startups for their knowledge of systematic methodologies, in this way creating hard empirical data which could be used for future research and to validate the results of this study.

Regarding **specialized media players,** both SSE's are even, with a moderate amount of local specialized media sources. Austria has 3, Switzerland has 3, positioning both in the 3-5 bracket, classifying as L2 for this factor. However, a data analysis can reveal how much local SSE members actually visit these websites. Using Amazon Alexa's Siteinfo tool (*Alexa*, n.d.) on the date of this research (December 2019), the global internet engagement ranking for the 6 listed media sites are the following:

Medium	Country	Ranking
FutureZone	Austria	#46,085
StartupTicker	Switzerland	#74,617
Der Brutkasten	Austria	#151,105
FintechNews	Switzerland	#245,763
Trending Topics	Austria	#350,393
Startwerk	Switzerland	#750,713

Table 4: Startup Media Players Global Engagement Rankings.

Averaging the rankings for both countries would result in a #182,527 rank for the Austrian local media players and a #357,031 for Switzerland's, with Austria's average surpassing that of Switzerland. Also, while StartupTicker as the Swiss top performer surpasses both Brutkasten and Trending Topics, it is surpassed by Austria's top performer FutureZone. Thus, while both countries are served by the same number of local startup media players and therefore have the same classification in this factor, a deeper analysis of the statistics shows that Austria's public is more engaged with these websites than their Swiss neighbors.

The following factors are relative to the SSE's population size.

The first of these is the **number of startups.** Before analyzing the results, it is important to clarify the methodology used. The description in the maturity model, which states that this factor measures the number of startups founded *by year,* is found to be incongruent with the results of the other existing case studies. Using the same data source as the authors (Crunchbase), neither Tel Aviv, nor São Paulo or New York reach their classifications for any recorded year, if measured by startups per year. However, measuring by total number of startups, the results match the classifications. Thus, this study is led to conclude that by number of startups, the model understands *total* number of startups relative to the SSE population. For this criterion, Zürich is classified as L3, while Vienna has a maturity level of L2. When it comes to yearly foundings, the Swiss SSE also comes ahead, with an average of 169 Startups founded in 2014-2016, while Vienna had 104. As such, Zürich surpasses Vienna both in absolute and in relative numbers, since the Austrian city is more populous than the Swiss canton. If is of note that Crunchbase data aligns with local startup reports: The ASM survey (Leitner et al. 2018) found that 50% of Austrian Startups were based in Vienna, close to the 51,71% of Crunchbase. Furthermore, the databases presented by Kyora et al. (2018) credited Zürich with headquartering 30,02% of Swiss Startups, also very close to the 29,31% of Crunchbase.

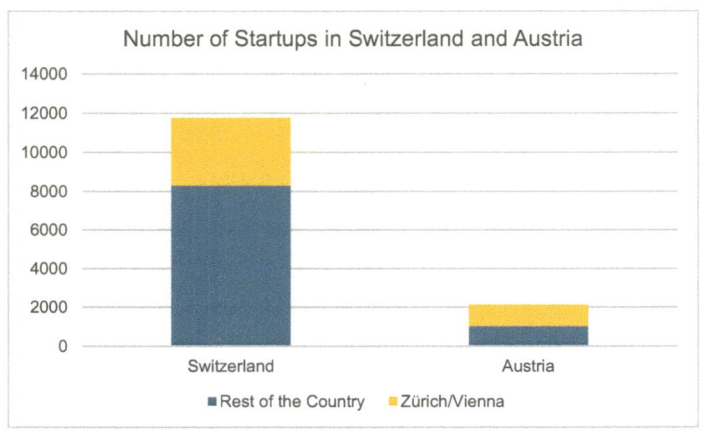

Figure 6: Number of Startups in Switzerland and Austria. Source: Crunchbase.

When it comes to **angel funding in number of deals/year,** Zürich has a number advantage over Vienna. According to Dealroom (*Dealroom.co*, n.d.), Zürich had 8 angel funding rounds in 2019, 5 in 2018, and 10 in 2017, a total of 23 over the last three years. In comparison, Vienna had 4 angel funding rounds in 2019, 1 in 2018 and 7 in 2017, a total of 12 over the last three years. As the data shows, Zürich had more angel deals every single year and in the three-year average, both in absolute and relative numbers, with a 91,6% higher number of deals on the three-year average than the Austrian capital.

Both SSE's fare well in **high-tech companies presence.** Vienna has a classification of L2 with 17 high-tech established companies (more on the definition under "Established Companies Influence"), while Zürich has a classification of L3 with 24 such companies having been found in total. The higher number of high-tech companies in the Swiss SSE can to some extent be attributed to the overall higher number of big companies in general which have headquarters in the region. According to *Startup Heatmap Report* (2019), both Vienna and Zürich have their strongest verticals in FinTech, with notable companies from the two cities being Raiffeisen and the SIX Group, respectively. When it comes to the global ecosystem, Switzerland has Zürich and Geneva as the world's 2nd and 3rd greatest Fintech hubs, while Austria has Vienna occupying the 15th position (Ankenbrand et al., 2019), showing that in this segment, both SSE's are world-class.

In **access to funding in number of deals/year,** a 54% difference between the two SSEs can be observed. While Vienna had in total 64 funding rounds, which classifies it as L1 for this factor, Zürich had in total 99 funding rounds, which earns it a classification of L2. Although Vienna is absolute numbers had less funding deals than Zürich (a 35 deals difference), the Austrian capital is responsible for a higher percentage of deals in its country than the Swiss canton. Austria in total had 101 deals, with Vienna being responsible for 63% of them, more than half of all deals. Meanwhile, Switzerland had 230 deals, with Zürich being responsible for 43% of them, showing like in "access to funding in USD/year" that the Swiss SSE is less centralized than the Austrian.

Regarding **incubators/tech parks,** both SSEs have many active support organizations of this kind. Vienna has a total of 10 of these, including some with worldwide networks and backing from multinational companies, such as the Global Incubator Network Austria. Large national companies also support these initiatives, with high-tech Frequentis having its own incubation program. In comparison to Vienna, Zürich again shows more development, with a total of 16 incubators/tech parks, 60% more than Vienna. The Zürich canton in particular is home to 3 of the 5 Swiss Technoparks, one in Zürich proper, one in Winterthur and one in Schlieren-Zürich, with backing from established banking institutions such as UBS, CreditSuisse and the Zürcher Kantonalbank. In any case, both SSE's rank L3 for this factor.

The last factor is **established companies influence,** which tracks the number of established companies that are actively engaged in nurturing the SSE. The term "established companies" which is also used for the factor "high-tech companies presence", refers to "big" companies in Cukier & Kon (2018), but does not exactly specify how big a "big" company is. When personally inquiring Dr. Cukier about this factor, the model's author replied that it is a subjective criterion that encompasses companies that have at least national impact. Using this description, a total of 16 companies were found in the Vienna region and 18 in the Zürich region, a 12,5% difference showing a slightly higher prevalence of influential established companies in the Swiss SSE. To make this criterion even more universally appliable and objective, a specific measurable metric could be defined, such as total assets in relation to the country's economy, to determine which companies count as established companies. Then, the companies which are considered established can be investigated in regard to their engagement and influence in the SSE.

Considering all **essential factors**, Zürich is slightly more mature than Vienna. The Swiss canton has five factors classified as L3 and five as L2, whilst Vienna has also four classified as L3, five as L3 and one as L1. Comparatively, both SSEs have equivalent maturity in exit strategies, global markets, entrepreneurship in universities (L3), culture values for entrepreneurship, ecosystem generations and number of startups (L2). Zürich is more mature in ecosystem data and research, high-tech company presence (L3 to L2), and angel funding in number of deals (L2 to L1). Meanwhile, Vienna is more mature in startup events (L3 to L2).

The **complementary factors** also demonstrate a higher maturity of Zürich's SSE. When compared, both SSEs have the same maturity level in mentoring quality, technology transfer processes, incubators/tech parks (L3), bureaucracy, specialized media players, methodologies knowledge, accelerators quality (L2) and human capital quality (L1). Zürich was found to be more mature in the factors established company presence (L3 to L2) tax burden (L3 to L1), and access to funding in USD as well as number of deals per year (L2 to L1). Vienna was not found to be more mature than Zürich in any of the complementary factors.

Finally, the **maturity level**. This section will be divided into two parts, one for each SSE, since the recommendations for each are different.

Vienna is considered to be a nascent ecosystem, with M1 maturity. For nascent ecosystems, Cukier & Kon (2018) identify the most important metrics to be entrepreneurship in universities, culture values for entrepreneurship and events. Vienna already has a strong event scene but can still work on culture values for entrepreneurship and entrepreneurship in universities. From the government's side, tax burden is the most pressing concern (currently L1), followed by bureaucracy. The general ecosystem is found to have quality institutions, but funding, both normal (L1) or angel (L1), is still lacking, or at least partly not made public. These are the most underdeveloped metrics, with angel funding being the only essential factor on L1. Thus, attracting more capital, along with developing angel networks, is vital for the ecosystem to mature.

Zürich is considered to be a mature ecosystem, with M3 maturity. For ecosystems in this stage, Cukier & Kon (2018) identify the most important metrics as being exit strategies, cultural values for entrepreneurship and specialized media. While the first is already well developed, since Switzerland has a strong M&A scene, work can still be done in spreading entrepreneurial culture and increasing the reach and number of startup media outlets. Contrary to Austria, the greater concern for the government is bureaucracy, since the tax regime is already favorable for entrepreneurship. The SSE was found to be overall well-developed, not falling behind starkly in any factor, with the exception of human capital quality, whose measurement was put into question. Secondary goals for the SSE include expanding entrepreneurship in universities, increasing angel funding as well as the amount of data, events and research on the ecosystem, and lastly engaging successful founders to support the next generation of entrepreneurs.

4.2. Comparison and Model Implications

This was the first application of the Software Startup Ecosystem maturity model in a European setting, since it so far had only been applied in Brazil, the US and Israel. It is also the second application of the model to a small country setting, since Israel, Austria and Switzerland have similar population and territorial sizes. It provided the first M1 classification (Vienna) and the first M3 classification (Zürich), with now at least one ecosystem in each maturity level (São Paulo is M2, Tel Aviv and New York are M4). Researchers which analyze other ecosystems will now have at least one case study of an ecosystem in that stage of evolution, irrespective of the maturity level.

The results of this study were also the most varied. So far, no ecosystem had different factor classifications in essential factors and none had factors in three different maturity levels for complementary factors. The latter for Switzerland is due to measurement issues, already discussed in the human capital quality factor, but overall it represents aspects of European startup ecosystems, which, from the factors analyzed, seem less uniform in their development. While the self-sustaining ecosystem of Tel-Aviv and New York have all essential factors in the most mature level of development and the evolving São Paulo has them all in L2, Vienna and Zürich have almost an even split of factors between maturity levels. This shows that, although both ecosystems are growing, not all areas are developing at the same pace.

A comparison to the results of the Tel Aviv classification also reveal similarities between its less mature European counterparts. Of the complementary 4 factors that didn't classify as L3, bureaucracy and specialized media are seen in the same levels in Zürich and Vienna, while a third factor, tax burden, is also a less developed factor in Vienna, although at another maturity level. Methodologies knowledge, on the other hand, is the only factor in which both Vienna and Zürich are more developed than Tel Aviv.

The course of this study also provided insights on the definition of software startup ecosystems itself. Most of the factors analyzed are not exclusive to software startups, but to startups in general. Only the factors "high-tech companies" presence and "technology transfer processes" can be said to be exclusive to tech startups, but even then, not all tech startups are software startups. Indeed, most events, accelerators, and funding networks are related to all startups. However, a significant part of the Zürich and Vienna ecosystems is focused on software and ICT, due to their strong software-intensive branches such as Fintech. As such, there also are programs focusing exclusively on tech startups, and Switzerland even has its own ICT-only investor network. So, while there is certainly overlap between the software startup ecosystem and the general ecosystem, there is also a distinguishable ICT/software segment.

In this sense, the software startup community is supported by both the broader ecosystem and the narrower software ecosystem. The SSE is a part of the broader startup ecosystem, being included in it along with other kinds of startups. This allows for different levels of analysis when studying the ecosystem, which can also be incorporated in the maturity model. Factors could be measured in total numbers and in relation to software startups where applicable. For example, number of startups and deals could be complemented by factors "number of ICT startups" and "number of ICT deals", providing an overview of the relative importance of the software component inside a startup ecosystem.

4.3. Conclusion

This bachelor thesis sought to analyze the software startup ecosystems of two regional startup hubs in Central Europe: Vienna, in Austria, and Zürich, in Switzerland. For this, the Software Startup Ecosystem maturity model (Cukier & Kon, 2018) was applied.

Differences and similarities between the two could be identified by maturity levels in individual factors. The results found the Viennese ecosystem to be nascent, already possessing well-developed factors, but still lacking in funding. Meanwhile, Zürich's ecosystem was classified as mature, almost reaching a level of self-sustainability.

The Swiss success case can show Austrian startup stakeholders a path in making their own software startup ecosystem more mature, especially in regard to its more undeveloped factor. Investors can study how the organization of Swiss investors focused on IT startups helped boost the ecosystem, while government agents can try to attract more investments by implementing more competitive tax models. Switzerland can also learn from its neighbor, for example, in giving startup ecosystem stakeholders a better overview of the event scene through advanced universal event platforms.

Through the course of this study, some improvement suggestions to the maturity model itself were developed, such as for the human capital quality factor. The aim of these suggestions is to help keep the model up-to-date and make it more objective and universally applicable, so that more case studies can be made and that their results be more easily replicable.

The results of this study were also compared with those of existing case studies, showing differences and similarities between the two European ecosystems and the three other analyzed before. This was followed by a discussion of the significance of the software startup ecosystem in relation to the broader startup ecosystem, based on the experience from this study, which resulted in a proposal for the inclusion of more software startup oriented metrics in the next versions of the model.

Further research could try to acquire more data from startups, universities and accelerators to increase the reliability of the metrics used in the two classifications. Lastly, global researchers creating reports on startup ecosystems could start including metrics for factors that are still hard to measure in the model, such as methodologies knowledge and mentoring quality, to make future comparisons between individual countries and SSEs easier

5. List of Tables

6. List of Figures

7. References

A1 Membership. (n.d.). *A1 Start Up Campus.* Retrieved January 11, 2020, from

> https://www.a1startup.net/en/a1-membership-en/

A1 Partnership. (n.d.). *A1 Start Up Campus.* Retrieved January 11, 2020, from

> https://www.a1startup.net/en/a1-partnership-en/

Acs, Z. J., Laszlo, S., Esteban, L., & Ainsley, L. (2018). *Global Entrepreneurship and*

> *Development Index 2018.* Springer International Publishing.

> https://www.springer.com/de/book/9783030032784

Alexa. (n.d.). Retrieved January 11, 2020, from https://www.alexa.com/siteinfo/

Ankenbrand, T., Dietrich, A., & Bieri, D. (2019). *IFZ FinTech Study 2019: An Overview of Swiss*

> *FinTech.* Institute of Financial Services, IFZ.

> https://blog.hslu.ch/retailbanking/files/2019/03/IFZ-FinTech-Study-2019_Switzerland.pdf

Austrian Tech Exit Report (p. 21). (2015). i5invest Beratungs GmbH.

> https://i5invest.com/news/austrian-tech-exit-report-2015/

Bandera, C., & Thomas, E. (2018). The role of innovation ecosystems and social capital in

> startup survival. *IEEE Transactions on Engineering Management, 66*(4), 542–551.

Bell-Masterson, J., & Stangler, D. (2015). Measuring an entrepreneurial ecosystem. *Available at SSRN 2580336.* http://utrechtce.nl/wp-content/uploads/2015/08/measuring_an_entrepreneurial_ecosystem.pdf

Biotech Cluster in Switzerland (Enabling New Business). (2019). Switzerland Global Enterprise. https://www.s-ge.com/sites/default/files/publication/free/factsheet-ict-switzerland-s-ge-en-2019.pdf

Blockchain Hub Switzerland (Enabling New Business). (2019). Switzerland Global Enterprise. https://www.s-ge.com/sites/default/files/publication/free/factsheet-blockchain-en-s-ge-2019.pdf

Business Navigator: Key Economic Figures about Switzerland. (n.d.). Switzerland Global Enterprise Business Navigator. Retrieved January 11, 2020, from https://business-navigator.s-ge.com

Company foundation in Switzerland. (n.d.). S-GE. Retrieved January 11, 2020, from https://www.s-ge.com/en/publication/fact-sheet/company-foundation-switzerland

Crunchbase. (n.d.). Retrieved January 11, 2020, from https://www.crunchbase.com/

CryptoValley Swiss Blockchain Ecosystem. (n.d.). CryptoValley Swiss Blockchain Ecosystem. Retrieved January 11, 2020, from http://cryptovalley.directory

Cukier, D., & Kon, F. (2018) A maturity model for software startup ecosystems. *Journal of Innovation and Entrepreneurship, 7*(1), 14.

Cukier, D., Kon, F., & Krueger, N. (2015). Designing a maturity model for software startup ecosystems. *International Conference on Product-Focused Software Process Improvement,* 600–606. https://link.springer.com/chapter/10.1007/978-3-319-26844-6_45

Cukier, D., Kon, F., & Lyons T. S. (2016). Software startup ecosystems evolution: The New York City case study *International Workshop on Software Startups.* http://ccsl.ime.usp.br/startups/sites/ccsl.ime.usp.br.startups/files/newyork-ecosystem.pdf

de Almeida, P. A. D., & de Almeida, S. J. (2019). The Belo Horizonte Software Startups Ecosystem and its maturity. *Proceedings of the XV Brazilian Symposium on Information Systems,* 1-8. https://dl.acm.org/doi/pdf/10.1145/3330204.3330262

Dealroom.co. (n.d.). Retrieved January 11, 2020, from https://app.dealroom.co/dashboard

Del Bosco, B., Mazzucchelli, A., Chierici, R., & Di Gregorio, A. (2019). Innovative startup

   creation: The effect of local factors and demographic characteristics of entrepreneurs.

   International Entrepreneurship and Management Journal, 1–20.

   https://link.springer.com/content/pdf/10.1007/s11365-019-00618-0.pdf

Discover: Einblicke in das Jahr 2018 von Innosuisse (p. 36). (2019). Innosuisse.

   https://issuu.com/innosuisse/docs/190325_innosuisse_bericht_2018_190x

Ecosystem Directory. (n.d.). *Swiss Finance + Technology Association*. Retrieved January 11,

   2020, from https://swissfinte.ch/institute/ecosystem-directory/

Ecosystem for start-ups in Vienna. (2019). Vienna Business Agency.

   https://viennabusinessagency.at/fileadmin/user_upload/Gruenden_und_Wachsen/OEkos

   ystem/Ecosystem_Englisch_-_2019September.pdf

Elevate Startup Acceleration. (n.d.). *TheVentury*. Retrieved January 11, 2020, from

   https://theventury.com/elevate/alumni/

Event Calendar. (n.d.). *AustrianStartups*. Retrieved January 11, 2020, from

   https://www.austrianstartups.com/events/

Eventbrite. (n.d.). Eventbrite. Retrieved January 11, 2020, from https://www.eventbrite.ch

Events Startupticker.ch. (n.d.). Retrieved January 11, 2020, from

   https://www.startupticker.ch/en/events

Fintech Switzerland (Enabling New Business). (2019). Switzerland Global Enterprise.

   https://www.s-ge.com/sites/default/files/publication/free/factsheet-fintech-switzerland-s-

   ge-en-2019.pdf

*Foster, G., Shimizu, C., Ciesinski, S., Davila, A., Hassan, S., Jia, N., & Morris, R. (2013).

   Entrepreneurial ecosystems around the globe and company growth dynamics. World

   Economic Forum, 1, 1-36.*

   http://www3.weforum.org/docs/WEF_EntrepreneurialEcosystems_Report_2013.pdf

Genome, S. (2012). *Global Startup Ecosystem Report 2012.*

   https://startupgenome.com/reports/global-startup-ecosystem-report-2012

Genome, S. (2017). *Global Startup Ecosystem Report 2017.*

   https://startupgenome.com/reports/global-startup-ecosystem-report-2017

Genome, S. (2019). *Global Startup Ecosystem Report 2019*.

    https://startupgenome.com/reports/global-startup-ecosystem-report-2019

Global market at a glance. (n.d.). *Startupticker*. Retrieved December 11, 2019, from

    https://www.startupticker.ch/en/facts/global-market-at-a-glance

Heimann, T., & Kyora, S. (2019). *Swiss Venture Capital Report*. Startupticker.ch.

    https://www.startupticker.ch/en/swiss-venture-capital-report

How to start a Business in Austria. (n.d.). Retrieved January 11, 2020, from

    https://investinaustria.at/en/starting-business/

Innovation Monitor. (n.d.). Retrieved January 11, 2020, from https://www.innovation-monitor.ch/

Kailer, N., Gutschelhofer, A. Abfalter, T., & Taferner, R. (2018). *Entrepreneurial intentions and*

    activities of students and their interrelation with entrepreneurship education: National

    Report Austria. Global University Entrepreneurial Spirit Students' Survey.

    http://guesssurvey.org/resources/nat_2018/GUESSS_Report_2018_Austria.pdf

Kandler, F. (2018). *Startup Report Austria 2018* (p. 61). https://www.startupreport.at/

Kickstart » Alumni. (n.d.). Retrieved January 11, 2020, from https://kickstart-

    innovation.com/alumni/

Kollmann, T., Stöckmann, C., Hensellek, S., & Kensbock, J. (2016). *European startup monitor*

    2016. Universität Duisburg-Essen Lehrstuhl für E-Business. https://duepublico2.uni-

    due.de/servlets/MCRFileNodeServlet/duepublico_derivate_00043444/ESM_2016.pdf

Krajcik, V., & Formanek, I. (2015). Regional Startup Ecosystem. *European Business &*

    Management, *1*(2), 14–18.

Kurth, L. (2019). *Clarity on Mergers & Acquisitions*. KPMG AG.

    https://assets.kpmg/content/dam/kpmg/ch/pdf/clarity-on-mergers-and-acquisitions-2019-

    en.pdf

Kyora, S., Rockinger, M., & Jondeau, E. (2018). *Swiss Startup Radar 2018/2019* (p. 106).

    Startupticker.ch.

    https://www.startupticker.ch/uploads/File/Attachments/StartupRadar_web.pdf

Leitner, K.-H., Dömötör, R., Raunig, M., & Zahradnik, G. (2018). *Austrian Startup Monitor*.

    http://austrianstartupmonitor.at/wp-content/uploads/2018/10/Austrian-

    StartUpMonitor2018_12MB.pdf

Motoyama, Y., & Watkins, K. K. (2014). Examining the Connections within the Startup Ecosystem: A case study of St. Louis. *Entrepreneurship Research Journal*, 7(1). https://core.ac.uk/download/pdf/75780609.pdf

Pandey, N. K. (2018). An Analysis of Startup Ecosystem in Metropolitan City in India. *International Journal of Engineering and Management Research (IJEMR)*, 8(2), 237–244.

Queirós, M., Braga, V., & Correia, A. (2019). Cross-country analysis to high-growth business: Unveiling its determinants. *Journal of Innovation & Knowledge*, 4(3), 146–153.

Schwab, K. (2017). Global Competitiveness Report 2017-2018. *World Economic Forum*. https://www.weforum.org/reports/the-global-competitiveness-report-2017-2018

Schwab, K. (2019). Global Competitiveness Report 2019. *World Economic Forum*. https://www.weforum.org/reports/global-competitiveness-report-2019

Sharma, S. K., & Meyer, K. E. (2019). New Startup Ecosystems and the Innovation Hub. In *Industrializing Innovation - the Next Revolution* (pp. 87–111). Springer. https://link.springer.com/chapter/10.1007/978-3-030-12430-4_8.

Sieger, P., Baldegger, R., & Fueglistaller, U. (2018). *Studentisches Unternehmertum in der Schweiz 2018*. Global University Entrepreneurial Spirit Students' Survey. http://guesssurvey.org/resources/nat_2018/GUESSS_Report_2018_Switzerland.pdf

Siegl, R. (2017a). *Why You Should Research in Austria: Industry 4.0* (Research Location Austria). Austrian Business Agency. https://investinaustria.at/en/downloads/brochures.php

Siegl, R. (2017b). *Why You Should Research in Austria: Information and Communications Technology* (Research Location Austria). Austrian Business Agency. https://investinaustria.at/en/downloads/brochures.php

Siegl, R. (2017c). *Why You Should Research in Austria: Life Sciences* (Research Location Austria). Austrian Business Agency. https://investinaustria.at/en/downloads/brochures.php

Siegl, R. (2017d). *Why You Should Research in Austria: Research Location Austria* (Research Location Austria). Austrian Business Agency. https://investinaustria.at/en/downloads/brochures.php

Siegl, R. (2019a). *Austria: Why you should set up your headquarters here*. Austrian Business Agency. https://investinaustria.at/en/downloads/brochures.php

Siegl, R. (2019b). *Startup Location Austria*. Austrian Business Agency. https://investinaustria.at/en/downloads/brochures/ABA-startups.pdf

Spin-off Information ETHZ, EPFL, PSI, WSL, Empa, Eawag. (n.d.). Spied. Retrieved January 11, 2020, from https://spied.ch/

Stam, E. (2018). Measuring entrepreneurial ecosystems. In: O'Connor A., Stam E., Sussan F., Audretsch D. (eds) *Entrepreneurial ecosystems* (pp. 173–197). Springer.

Startup Ecosystem Rankings (p. 158). (2019). StartupBlink. https://report.startupblink.com/

Startup Heatmap Report (p. 44). (2019). Startup Heatmap Europe. https://www.startupheatmap.com/download-reports/

Startup.ch. (n.d.). Retrieved January 11, 2020, from https://www.startup.ch/index.cfm?page=129571

Startups. (n.d.). WeXelerate Retrieved January 11, 2020, from https://www.wexelerate.com/ecosystem/startups/

Subrahmanya, M. B. (2017). Comparing the Entrepreneurial Ecosystems for Technology Startups in Bangalore and Hyderabad, India. *Technology Innovation Management Review*, 7(7).

Swiss Startups—Venturelab. (n.d.). Retrieved January 11, 2020, from https://www.venturelab.ch/index.cfm?cftoken=d351514e509e6d77-D1B8F7C5-ADEB-4240-207B9335FC02DE5D&cfid=303544885&page=137241&form_done=8812#fgFormAnker_8812

Swiss Tech Startup Ecosystem. (2019). Swiss ICT Investor Club. https://www.sictic.ch/map/

SwissStartups.org. (n.d.). Retrieved January 11, 2020, from http://www.swissstartups.org/

Switzerland—A Hub for Robotics and Drones (Enabling New Business). (2019). Switzerland Global Enterprise. https://www.s-ge.com/sites/default/files/publication/free/robotics_drones_en_0.pdf

Switzerland—ICT Business Location (Enabling New Business). (2019). Switzerland Global

   Enterprise. https://www.s-ge.com/sites/default/files/publication/free/factsheet-ict-

   switzerland-s-ge-en-2019.pdf

Tripathi, N., Oivo, M., Liukkunen, K., & Markkula, J. (2019). Startup ecosystem effect on

   minimum viable product development in software startups. *Information and Software*

   Technology, 114, 77-91.

Tripathi, N., Seppänen, P., Boominathan, G., Oivo, M., & Liukkunen, K. (2019). Insights into

   startup ecosystems through exploration of multi-vocal literature. *Information and*

   Software Technology, 105, 56–77.

Unterkalmsteiner, M., Abrahamsson, P., Wang, X., Nguyen-Duc, A., Shah, S., Bajwa, S. S.,

   Baltes, G. H., Conboy, K., Cullina, E., & Dennehy, D. (2016). Software startups–a

   research agenda. *E-Informatica Software Engineering Journal, 10*(1).

8. Appendix

Appendix 1: Template Email

Dear [ORGANIZATION NAME / PERSON NAME],

My name is Francisco Litvay, and I am a Business Informatics student in the Johannes Kepler University in Linz. I'm currently doing my Bachelor thesis on the Software Startup Ecosystem Maturity of Vienna and Zürich, comparing the Austrian and Swiss Ecosystems utilizing a model already applied in Israel, Brazil and the US. I hope my findings will help assess the weaknesses and strengths of our ecosystem and how we can improve, providing insights to the whole software startup community.

Because of that, it would be of an immense help if you could help me with any of the following data points from your organization's experience. In case not, I would appreciate it if you would be able to point me in the right direction (other sources or people to get in touch with).

- [FACTOR NAME] – [FACTOR DEFINITION]
- [EXAMPLE: Mentoring quality—The percentage of mentors that fit one of these criteria: (1) had a successful startup in the past and (2) founded and worked for more than 10 years in one or more startups.]
- [...]

Both percentage as well as total numbers would be most welcome.

Thanks in advance and best regards,
Francisco Litvay